Minnesota

• Moorhead

Brainerd•

Duluth •

Minneapolis• ★ St. Paul

Rochester•

 **is for**
Minnesota

written by kids
for kids

WESTWINDS
PRESS®

A

is for **Apple**

Honeycrisp apples, so crunchy and sweet.
They are my favorite fruit to eat.

B

is for

Boundary
Waters

In the Boundary Waters
on a sunny day,
You may see otters
splash and play.

C is for
Cherry on a Spoon

Big fat cherry on a spoon,
Round and red like a balloon.

D

is for

Dogsledding

Teams of dogs run
through snow,
Taking mushers where
they want to go.

E is for Entertainment

At Mall of America there's so much to do:
An aquarium, a theme park, and tons of stores, too.

F is for **Farming**

Minnesota farmers grow many useful crops.
Corn, soybeans, oats, and sugar beets are tops.

G is for **Gray Wolf**

Gray wolves on the move, pups in tow,
Through deciduous forests hunting prey as they go.

H

is for **Hockey**

Many Minnesota players who skate in our games
Go on to have careers full of fame.

I is for Ice House

In an ice house I gave fishing a try,
And before long I caught a walleye.

J

is for Jell-O Salad

Of all the sweets I've found in Jell-O,
My favorite by far is the marshmallow.

K

is for Kayaking

When kayaking it's fun to explore
All our lakes, even Lake Superior.

L

is for **Loon**

If you want to find a loon
Listen for its beautiful tune.

M

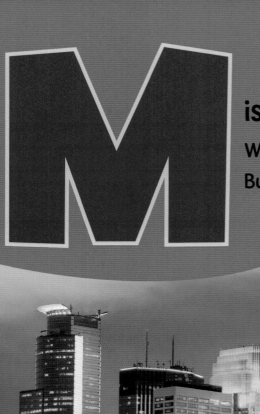

is for **Minneapolis**

We used to be the city that milled all the flour,
But now there's hustle and bustle every hour!

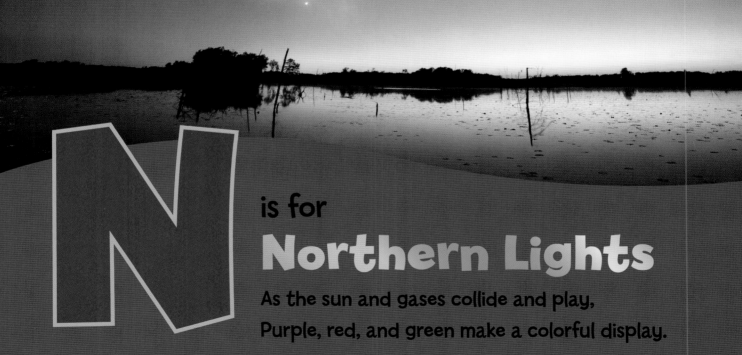

N is for
Northern Lights

As the sun and gases collide and play,
Purple, red, and green make a colorful display.

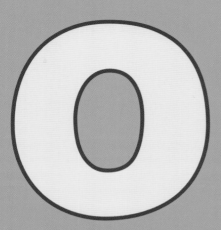

O

is for **Ojibwe**

Anishinaabe, Ojibwe, and Chippewa are all one nation.
They came to Minnesota in a westward migration.

P is for Prairies

Grass so tall, expanse so vast—
I've come to see the prairie at last.

Q is for **Queen**

Who is bigger, better, *butter*?
At the State Fair we all love her.

R

is for **Raptors**

The Raptor Center's innovation
Helps many birds to rehabilitation.

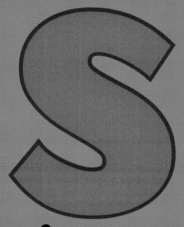

S

is for
St. Paul

Minneapolis's twin is
historic St. Paul.
From the capitol to museums—
hop the light rail to see it all.

T

is for **Tubing**

In Minnesota you can have fun in the snow
And then go home and make hot cocoa!

U

is for **Up North**

Winter or summer, cabin or tent,
Snowshoeing or fly fishing . . .
whatever's your bent.

V

is for **Vikings**

Skol Vikings, let's go!

Watch them score,

Then hear the fans let out a roar.

W

is for

Walleye

We spend time on the water
making just one wish:
"Please let me catch our
great state fish."

X is for **X-treme Sports**

You have to be adventurous to do extreme sports.
Ice cross and bungee jumping are not played on courts.

is for
You Betcha

In Minnesota we are friendly
in our own unique way.
You will hear
"Ya sure, you betcha"
every single day.

Z is for **Zoo**

See penguins wobble and seals splash,
Watch the monkeys dart and dash.

Who Knew?

Apple
More than thirty apple varieties are grown in Minnesota. The Honeycrisp is the state fruit and was first developed at the University of Minnesota in the 1960s. It is prized for its crisp texture and sweet-tart flavor. Yum!

Boundary Waters
This million-acre wilderness in northern Minnesota is made up of 1,000-plus lakes, waterways, and bogs. It's a popular destination for camping, fishing, and canoeing. It has the highest point in Minnesota (2,300-foot Eagle Mountain) and some of the oldest rock in North America (2.7 billion-year-old greenstone lava)!

Cherry on a Spoon
The giant spoon in *Spoonbridge and Cherry* weighs 5,800 pounds and stretches fifty-two feet across a pond. The cherry weighs 1,200 pounds and sprays water out its stem! It's the highlight of the Minneapolis Sculpture Garden. Minnesotans are big art supporters: 95 percent believe the arts should be a part of children's education.

Dogsledding
Dogsledding is popular in northern Minnesota. The sled driver is called a musher, the dog at the front is the lead dog, and then come the point dogs, swing dogs, and finally the wheel dogs. Humans and dogs have been working together in snow for thousands of years.

Entertainment
There's plenty of entertainment at Mall of America—it's the largest mall in the US. There are more than 520 stores, 50 restaurants, the Nickelodeon Universe theme park, and an aquarium! With 40 million visitors each year, it's one of the most popular tourist destinations in the world.

Farming
Minnesota has almost 75,000 farms covering half its land. Corn and soybeans are the biggest crops, but it's also the top US grower of sugar beets, oats, sweet corn, and green peas. Hogs are the #1 animal, but farmers also raise turkeys, elk, bison, and even ostriches!

Gray Wolf
Gray wolves once roamed the US, but in the 1800s they were hunted to extinction in every state except Alaska and Minnesota, which now has a sustainable but threatened population. Wolves are important for a healthy forest habitat—they keep deer and elk populations in check, so they don't eat too much understory.

Hockey
Minnesota is the State of Hockey for good reason. Over 50,000 kids play—more than any other state—and the Minnesota Wild draws nearly 20,000 fans per game. Historians aren't sure where it came from, but we do know the first indoor ice hockey game happened in Canada in 1875. And the first pucks were frozen cow patties!

Facts about the

Ice House

Ice houses give shelter for ice fishing. Most are basic, but some have satellite TVs, bathrooms, and comfy beds! To ice fish you need special gear, too: an auger to cut a hole in the ice and a skimmer (large metal spoon with holes) to remove new ice that forms over the hole. And don't forget your heater!

Jell-O Salad

This traditional Minnesota side dish is Jell-O mixed with other foods—anything from shredded carrots and mandarin oranges to ham and cabbage. Jell-O was created in 1845 and originally came in just four flavors—lemon, orange, strawberry, and raspberry. Flavors that weren't so popular? Pineapple-grapefruit, celery, and tomato.

Kayaking

Minnesota is the Land of 10,000 Lakes. That's a lot of water for kayaking! Kayak means "hunter's boat" and was first used thousands of years ago by native peoples of the north for hunting, fishing, and transportation. Those kayaks had bone or driftwood frames with seal or caribou skins stretched over them. Today's kayaks are made of fiberglass or plastic.

Loon

The state bird is built like a torpedo, swimming under water to catch food. It's known for its call, but it actually has four. The tremolo sounds like crazy laughing, the wail is longer, the hoot is shorter, and the yodel is for males guarding territory. Minnesota has more loons than any other state except Alaska.

Minneapolis

Minneapolis and St. Paul were dubbed "the Twin Cities" by writer Mark Twain. Minneapolis was also called "Mill City" because 135 years ago it was the flour milling capital of the world! Maybe they should have called it "Candy City"—Mars Inc., makers of the Milky Way, Snickers, and M&Ms, was started there.

Northern Lights

Minnesota is one of the few states where you can see this dazzling light show (also called aurora borealis). It happens when charged particles from the sun's solar wind hit Earth's magnetic field. Different elements in our atmosphere make the colors. Oxygen makes green, nitrogen blue or red, and helium blue or purple.

Ojibwe

Ojibwe and Dakota are the main Native American groups in Minnesota today. But before European settlement, the state was home to many groups: Arapaho, Cheyenne, Fox and Sauk, Iowa, Omaha, Oto, Ottawa, Ponca, Winnebago, and Huron. Even the state name comes from a Dakota word meaning "sky-tinted water."

Prairies

Before European settlement, 18 million acres of prairie covered Minnesota. Now the native tallgrass prairie is the most endangered ecosystem in North America. Less than 2 percent remains. Prairies are home to many plants and animals, including badgers, coyotes, swift foxes, ferrets, prairie dogs, jackrabbits, and bison.

Queen

She's not really a queen—Minnesotans call her "Princess Kay of the Milky Way" and she's crowned every year at the Minnesota State Fair. But forget the crown—the winner (and even the runners-up) gets her likeness carved into a ninety-pound chunk of butter. Beautiful AND delicious!

great state of Minnesota

Raptors

Raptors are birds that hunt other animals. The Raptor Center, founded in 1974, is part of the University of Minnesota College of Veterinary Medicine. The center studies environmental issues affecting raptor health. They also rehabilitate 700 sick and injured raptors each year—hawks, falcons, kestrels, owls, eagles, and more.

St. Paul

The capital of Minnesota was once called Pig's Eye, after a popular tavern owner. The first Catholic pastor to arrive decided that wouldn't do and changed it to St. Paul. The city hosts the Winter Carnival, featuring a parade, treasure hunt. and ice-sculpting contests. Some years there's even an ice palace!

Tubing

Minnesota is hard to beat for winter sports. With five or more months of snow, that's a lot of time for cross-country and downhill skiing, snowboarding, tubing, ice fishing, snowmobiling . . . the list goes on and on. So pull on your snowsuit and get outside!

Up North

This term refers to any area an hour or more outside the Twin Cities where there are cabins on a lake. It can be north, south, east, or west. Up North is where Minnesotans go to enjoy the scenery while fishing, canoeing, water-skiing, and more.

Vikings

Minnesota's pro football team got its start in the NFL in 1961. Although they've made it to four Super Bowls without winning the championship (yet), they make the top ten for teams with the highest winning percentages in the league. Their name reflects Minnesota's Scandinavian heritage. Skol Vikings!

Walleye

The state fish is also its most popular, due to its yummy taste. Their large reflective eyes are light sensitive, so they swim in the deep waters by day and move to shallower waters at night. They have a mouth full of sharp teeth, so if you catch one, watch your fingers!

X-treme Sports

It's a great state for thrill seekers. Mountain biking, white-water kayaking, rock climbing, windsurfing, and more. Heck, you can even scuba dive in abandoned mine pits! But the craziest sport? Ice cross downhill. Held in St. Paul, skaters race down an icy walled track filled with sharp turns, treacherous jumps, and belly-churning drops. It's the fastest sport on ice!

You Betcha

Minnesota is full of interesting words and phrases. This one means you agree with someone. Other Minnesota-isms are "Uff-da," a Norwegian phrase expressing surprise or exhaustion, and "Dontcha know," which is tacked on to the end of a sentence to see if the listener understands. Got it? You betcha!

Zoo

The Minnesota Zoo first opened in Apple Valley in 1978 and is now home to more than 4,700 animals. The zoo is involved in conservation projects with moose, bison, and other native wildlife. They also coordinate tiger and Asian wild horse breeding programs to help protect these endangered species.

Thank you to the participants of the Jewish Big Brother/Big Sister Program at Jewish Family and Children's Service of Minneapolis (JFCS), who contributed the beautiful poetry for this book. **Way to go!** Thank you to the program's staff members Danielle Livon-Bemel, Carole Cera, Bobbie Goldfarb, and Shira Lavintman as well as Big Sisters Bette Goodman and Jen Friedman, who guided the youth through this process.

JFCS' Jewish Big Brother/Big Sister Program celebrated its 40th anniversary in 2015. It empowers Jewish children in need of a special friendship and their families by providing unconditional, personally matched Jewish mentoring relationships.

The Authors of *M is for Minnesota*

Gabby Evans (B)	Lia Harel (H, J, L, M, R)	Talia Malka (N, S, U, Z)
Ellie Fishman (K, Q, T, V)	Izzy Hazlett (A, P)	Ari Vlodaver (N)
Adina Gepner (K, Q, T, V)	Sam Hazlett (A, P)	Josie Wartnick (F, W, X, Y)
Yael Gepner (J, L, M, R)	Stephanie Israel (C, D, O)	Isaac Woodman (E, G, I)
Isabel Goldfarb (C, D, O)	Mira Malka (N, S, U, Z)	

Library of Congress Cataloguing-in-Publication Data
M is for Minnesota / written by kids for kids.
        pages cm. — (See-my-state series)
 Audience: Age 4–8.
 Audience: Grade K to grade 3.
 ISBN 978-1-943328-07-9 (hardcover)
 ISBN 978-1-943328-31-4 (e-book)
 1. Minnesota—Juvenile literature. 2. Alphabet books—Juvenile literature. I. McCann, Michelle Roehm, 1968- editor.
F606.3.M215 2016
977.6—dc23
                        2015034589

Editor: Michelle McCann
Designer: Vicki Knapton

Published by WestWinds Press®
An imprint of

P.O. Box 56118
Portland, Oregon 97238-6118
503-254-5591
www.graphicartsbooks.com

Printed in China

**Part of the growing See-My-State Series,
Written by Kids for Kids!**